A COLLECTION OF SELF LOVE POEMS

BLOOM

WRITTEN BY
DINA EZZEDDINE

Bloom
© 2024 Dina Ezzeddine

All rights reserved.

No part of this book may be reproduced, stored in a retrieval system, or transmitted in any form or by any means—electronic, mechanical, photocopy, recording, or otherwise—without prior written permission of the author, except in the case of brief quotations embodied in critical articles or reviews.

This book is a work of poetry. Names, characters, places, and incidents are the product of the author's imagination or are used fictitiously. Any resemblance to actual persons, living or dead, is purely coincidental.

Second Edition

ISBN: 978-1-0690893-2-8 (PAPERBACK)
ISBN: 978-1-0690893-3-5 (HARDCOVER)
ISBN 2: 979-8-3092183-2-5 (HARDCOVER EDITION 2)

"Through every hardship, may you find the strength to grow, the courage to heal, and the light to embrace all that you are becoming"

-with love, DEE

A COLLECTION OF SELF LOVE POEMS
BLOOM

CONTENTS

SEEDS OF BECOMING
exploring the beginnings of self-discovery and acceptance.

TENDER ROOTS
focusing on nurturing inner growth and resilience.

UNBREAKABLE LIGHT
poems about embracing inner strength and finding joy.

UNVEILED
reflecting on vulnerability, self-compassion, and authenticity.

WHOLE & FREE
celebrating the journey towards self-love and personal liberation.

SEEDS OF BECOMING

BEGINNINGS

You start small,
a whisper beneath the noise,
a single breath,
unfolding.

In the silence of growth,
there is a trembling,
a quiet rise,
a seed pressing upward—
unyielding,
toward light.

PERMISSION

Today, give yourself permission
to be imperfect, unfinished,
the sketch before the masterpiece.
Let the lines waver,
the colors spill
beyond borders.

You are not bound
by polished edges—
you are allowed to be
a work in progress.

ROOTS OF CHANGE

Not everything you plant
will bloom the same way—
some seeds push up fiercely,
others take time,
hidden in the earth,
before they see the sun.

Let yourself be both,
patient and wild,
rooted and reaching,
growing in your own time.

BECOMING

You do not need to rush—
each leaf, each petal,
knows the path of its unfolding.
Hold space for yourself,
for the mess,
the fragile, the unsure.
Becoming isn't always beautiful,
but it is always true.

THE FIRST BREATH

There is a spark,
a tender breath,
a flame that knows
no fear.

In that first inhalation,
you are infinite—
new and boundless,
untouched by doubt,
ready to become.

PATIENCE

Growth does not demand speed.
It arrives in seasons,
whispering,
wait for me.

Trust that your roots
know the way,
that each pause, each stillness,
holds a story
waiting to bloom.

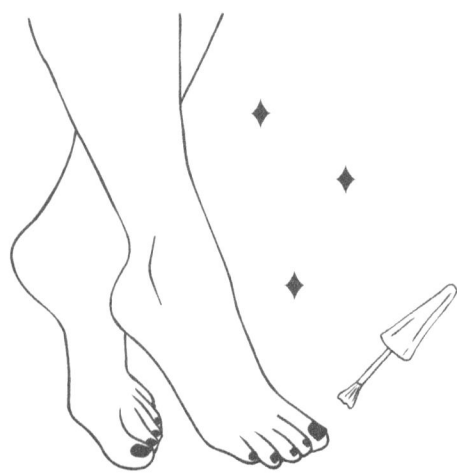

SELF-TENDER

Be soft with yourself,
as you would a blooming rose—
handle gently the parts
unfurling in their own time.

Hold this becoming
as if it were a secret,
a treasure that only you
are meant to cherish.

AWAKENING

Somewhere inside,
a light flickers,
the beginning of knowing,
of remembering—
you are enough
just as you are.

Each day, stoke that flame,
let it warm your bones,
remind you of the truth
that has been there all along.

FIRST BLOSSOMS

You may feel delicate,
as if the world is too strong,
too loud.

But in your softness,
there is a resilience,
a courage to rise,
to reach beyond fear.

And with each step,
you are blooming.

UNSEEN ROOTS

What grows beneath the surface,
the roots tangled, unseen,
are part of the becoming too.

Honor the hidden work,
the silent struggles,
the quiet days.

For even in darkness,
you are growing.

UNFOLDING

Do not rush the opening—
let each layer, each petal,
find its place in the light.

Be at ease in the slowness,
the quiet revolution
of becoming more
than you were yesterday.

THE JOURNEY

Becoming isn't always straight;
it curves, dips, and meanders.

Sometimes, it feels like a step back,
but know, dear soul,
you are moving forward
in ways you cannot yet see.

EMBRACE THE UNKNOWN

Let yourself lean into the mystery,
for there is beauty in not knowing,
a certain magic in becoming
what you have yet to understand.

In each uncertain step,
you find yourself.

GROWTH

To grow is to stretch,
to reach for places unseen,
to be patient with your own pace.

Remember: growth does not demand
a witness or applause—
it is its own quiet miracle.

WHISPERS OF CHANGE

Not all growth is loud—
sometimes, it's the quiet shift,
the soft unfolding within,
a whisper that says,
"Today, I will be kinder to myself."

TRUSTING IN TIME

Allow time to do its work,
for seeds don't rush to bloom.
In the waiting, you find
a patience that only comes
from trusting yourself to grow.

THE FIRST STEP

Be brave enough
to take that first step,
even if it trembles,
even if it feels small.
Every journey begins
with one moment of courage.

UNSEEN BEAUTY

In the soil, where no eyes can see,
your roots are weaving a story.
You may feel hidden now,
but you are preparing to rise
to the light, when it's time.

SELF-BELONGING

Today, belong to yourself,
claim each part,
the lost, the found, the in-between.
You are a mosaic
of every moment that brought you here.

IN EVERY BREATH

Becoming isn't always grand—
sometimes it's in the breaths
you take to steady yourself,
the moments you choose
to keep going, quietly.

INVISIBLE THREADS

There are pieces of you
woven into each step,
each gentle act of growth.
They hold you together
even on the days you feel undone.

BELIEF IN BLOOM

Believe in your own blooming,
even if today feels quiet,
even if you're not yet sure
what you'll become.
Your becoming is a promise
to yourself.

SMALL STEPS

Every step you take,
no matter how small,
plants a seed of courage.
Let it grow slowly,
a quiet victory
in each stride forward.

RECLAIMING

Take back the pieces of yourself
you once gave away.
Let them find new roots
in your heart,
growing strong
and full of life.

INWARD BLOOM

Sometimes the biggest bloom
is unseen—
a quiet shift inside,
a new way of seeing yourself
with tenderness,
with patience.

BEGINNINGS IN SILENCE

In the quiet, seeds stir,
finding life beneath the surface.
Not all beginnings are loud—
some rise softly,
a gentle promise to grow.

BECOMING FROM WITHIN

Your journey begins inward,
where roots of courage find strength.
Becoming is not about reaching out;
it's about discovering
the boundless within.

GROWTH WITHOUT HURRY

You are allowed to take your time.
Growth does not demand urgency—
it calls for patience,
a slow, steady bloom
from deep within.

TENDER ROOTS

ROOTS OF RESILIENCE

You are stronger than you know,
roots woven deep, unseen.
In each trial, you find more strength,
more depth to hold you steady
when the storms come.

GENTLE WITH GROWTH

Growth isn't just grand gestures—
it's the small kindnesses,
the quiet promises kept to yourself.
Tender roots, watered daily,
become forests in time.

LEARNING TO HOLD

To be soft does not mean
to be weak;
it is the art of holding,
of allowing pain to pass through,
of healing gently, from within.

WHEN YOU FALL

Not all falls are defeats.
Some are invitations to rest,
to remember that roots deepen
when you lean into the ground,
when you pause and begin again.

EMBRACE THE SOIL

You grow in the dirt,
not in the light alone.
There is beauty in the dark spaces,
where roots find their grip,
where life takes hold.

SAFE SPACES

Build a home within yourself—
a place to return
when the world feels too much,
a sanctuary of quiet
that only you can tend.

KINDNESS FOR THE SELF

Be kind, as you would to a flower
just starting to bloom.
Speak softly to the parts
that are still learning,
still growing, still becoming.

INNER GARDEN

Plant joy in your heart,
water it with laughter,
with care.
You are a garden,
a keeper of beauty
that needs time to grow.

SOFT POWER

Strength doesn't need to roar.
Sometimes it is soft,
a whisper of "I can,"
a gentle resilience
that keeps going quietly.

THE QUIET WORK

Not all growth is visible;
some of it happens
in the silences,
the pauses, the breaths
that steady your heart
and prepare it to soar.

ROOTS INTERTWINED

As you nurture yourself,
you'll find the threads
that connect you to others.
Your roots may be separate,
but the earth beneath
is shared.

SELF-COMPASSION

Forgive yourself daily,
for the mistakes, the doubts.
Like roots winding back,
your tenderness with yourself
only deepens your strength.

TEND TO THE WOUNDS

Healing is not about erasing,
but understanding,
letting each scar remind you
of how far you've come,
how each wound is a root
of your becoming.

QUIET CONFIDENCE

Grow softly,
without the need to be seen.
True confidence is knowing
you are whole,
even in solitude,
even in silence.

SEASONS OF GROWTH

Like the trees, you have seasons—
times to bloom,
and times to fall away,
to root deeper,
knowing the next spring
is yours to hold.

SLOWLY, SURELY

Growth doesn't rush;
it trusts in its own rhythm.
Like the roots that spread,
you, too, are growing
at the perfect pace.

UNSHAKEABLE

With roots strong and sure,
you learn to sway with storms,
bend without breaking.
There is a strength
in knowing you'll remain.

RETURN TO YOURSELF

You don't need to chase—
sometimes the greatest journey
is the return,
coming back to the quiet truths
you held all along.

TENDER STRENGTH

You don't have to be fierce
to be powerful.
In your gentleness,
there is a power
that heals,
that brings light to dark places.

STRENGTH IN SILENCE

Even in silence,
your roots reach down deep,
finding strength in stillness,
in the quiet resolve
to keep growing,
to keep pushing forward.

GENTLE PERSISTENCE

Growth doesn't always roar;
sometimes it whispers,
a gentle persistence
like roots finding their way
through rock and soil,
quiet but unstoppable.

SAFE SOIL

Find the soil that nurtures you,
the space where you feel held.
It's here, in safe spaces,
where your roots deepen,
where growth feels like home.

UNBREAKABLE LIGHT

UNBREAKABLE LIGHT

There is a light within you,
unchanged by time,
untouched by doubt.
It shines through every shadow,
a constant, a promise,
a quiet strength.

RADIANT IN SOLITUDE

In the silence of your own company,
find the warmth that only you can give.
Be your own sun,
your own safe haven,
a light bright enough
to fill the whole room.

MORNING JOY

Wake with the light
of knowing you are enough—
no additions, no approvals,
just the simple beauty
of your own existence.

GLOW

You don't need anyone
to turn on your light.
You are radiant,
a sun in your own sky,
capable of warming even
the coldest of days.

UNSEEN BRILLIANCE"

You may not see it,
but others feel the warmth
of your presence,
the way you light up
just by being true.

UNSHAKEN

Let life shake you,
but hold onto the core
that remains steady,
the part of you
that never dims
under any storm.

LUMINOUS HEART

Your heart beats with light,
a steady rhythm of love,
of courage, of hope.
Let it be a beacon
for the times
when the road feels dark.

ENDLESS GLOW

You are not a flicker;
you are a steady flame,
an endless glow that does not tire,
that does not dim
even in the longest nights.

GOLDEN MOMENTS

Find the gold in small moments—
a laugh, a breeze, a gentle breath.
These are the beams
that build your light,
that remind you of the warmth
that lives within.

A SUN INSIDE

Carry a sun inside you,
bright enough to withstand
any winter, any night.
This is your unbreakable light,
an everlasting warmth.

STRENGTH IN SOFTNESS

You don't need armor;
your softness is enough.
There is strength in being gentle,
in allowing yourself to shine
without hard edges.

WHOLE AND GLOWING

You don't need to seek completion—
you are whole,
a complete circle of light,
enough to fill yourself
and shine outward.

LIGHT AND SHADOW

Even in your shadows,
there is light.
A warmth exists
in the parts of you
that are learning, healing,
becoming.

LIGHTHOUSE HEART

Be your own guide,
a steady light on stormy nights.
You are a lighthouse
that stands for yourself,
anchored and bright.

UNSEEN SUNSHINE

Know that you radiate,
even when you can't see it.
Others feel the warmth
of your spirit,
the way you brighten rooms
just by being.

INNER GLOW

Not every light is meant to shine outward;
some are quiet glows,
an inner peace that needs no witness
but your own heart.

LIGHT FOR DARK DAYS

There will be dark days,
but know this:
your light is resilient,
capable of breaking through
even the heaviest clouds.

RADIANCE OF TRUTH

There will be dark days,
but know this:
your light is resilient,
capable of breaking through
even the heaviest clouds.

HOME IN LIGHT

Build a home in your light,
a place where you can rest,
warm and safe,
held by the glow
you create within.

THE BRIGHTEST FLAME

The brightest light
isn't always the loudest;
it's the steady glow,
the quiet certainty
that you are enough.

INNER HORIZON

Look within
to find new horizons,
brightened by your courage,
illuminated by the light
that has always been yours.

SUNLIT COURAGE

Move forward
with the courage of light,
bold enough to shine,
gentle enough to heal.

ANCHORED

Find your anchor,
the steady place within,
the root that holds you
through any storm,
strong and tender,
unwavering and true.

HEALING SOIL

There is healing
in the soil of your own soul,
a gentle nourishment
that feeds the roots
you've planted with love.

GROWING SOFTLY

Let yourself grow softly,
without the need to rush.
Tender roots find their way,
unrushed, unpressured,
becoming strong
in their own time.

UNVEILED

UNVEILING

Peel back each layer
like petals of a flower,
revealing the heart of you—
soft, tender,
yet strong enough to bloom.

BARE AND BRAVE

There is courage in baring
the truest parts of you,
in standing without disguise,
letting the world see
all that you are,
unafraid of the light.

NOTHING HIDDEN

Today, let yourself be seen—
each scar, each dream,
each quiet hope.
The world needs your honesty,
the way your truth
lights up the dark.

WHOLE

You are not just the best of you,
but every forgotten part,
every fragile piece.
In being whole, you are unveiled,
perfectly incomplete,
beautiful in your becoming.

SOFT ARMOR

Lay down the armor
you built to keep safe.
You don't need to be hard
to be strong;
in gentleness, there is power.

UNMASKED

You don't need the mask today.
Let the world see you—
beautifully flawed,
courageously open,
real in every way.

HOLDING THE FRAGILE

In every delicate part of you,
there is strength.
In each vulnerability,
you hold the power
to rise again,
to remain whole.

THE RAW TRUTH

Truth isn't always pretty—
sometimes it's raw,
worn down and weary.
But there is beauty
in showing up as you are,
real and unfiltered.

UNFOLDING

Be gentle with yourself
as you unfold,
revealing layer by layer,
learning to love
the beauty of every part
you once hid away.

TRUE COLORS

No need to hide today.
Let your true colors shine,
the bright, the dark,
the in-between.
They are all yours,
each hue a testament
to your journey.

SOFT EDGES

You don't need sharp edges
to protect yourself.
Let your softness be your strength,
a gentle resolve
to remain open
in a world that demands walls.

TRUSTING YOURSELF

In the mirror, look close.
See the parts
you once denied,
embrace each one
and know: you are enough,
as you are, unveiled.

VULNERABLE AND VALIANT

To be vulnerable is to be brave,
to show the parts of you
that are still learning to trust,
still healing, still growing.
In this, there is courage.

WITHOUT PRETENSES

Today, put down the act,
let yourself breathe,
be fully, honestly you—
the realness
you've been holding back.

HONEST EYES

Look at yourself with honest eyes,
see every flaw, every line,
not as something to hide
but as pieces of a story
that only you can tell.

HEART ON DISPLAY

Wear your heart
where the world can see—
not for approval,
but for the freedom
of being known,
of being true.

PEELING AWAY

Every day, peel away a layer—
the fear, the shame, the doubt.
Let yourself emerge,
new and unafraid,
radiant in your own skin.

TRUE TO YOU

Let no one else define you.
Be true to yourself,
to the parts only you know.
In this authenticity,
there is peace,
there is strength.

HELD BY HONESTY

Be honest with yourself,
for in each truth,
you find freedom.
Let your own heart
be the place
you feel most at home.

NAKED TRUTH

Strip away expectations,
the need to please.
Stand as you are,
raw, real, enough.
Your naked truth
is your greatest beauty.

LEARNING TO BE SEEN

Let go of the shadows,
the places you once hid.
Learn to be seen,
to let others witness
the light that lives
within your truest self.

ROOTS OF SELF

Know yourself fully,
not as the world sees,
but as you are in silence,
in solitude, in truth.
These are the roots
that hold you steady.

WHOLE & FREE

WHOLE AND FREE

To be whole is to be free,
unbound by fear,
complete in every flaw and strength,
a harmony of light and shadow.

TRUE FREEDOM

Freedom isn't found in perfection
but in loving every piece,
even the scars, even the tender places
you once kept hidden.

COMPLETE IN MY OWN SKIN

I am no longer seeking pieces,
no longer reaching for more.
I am whole as I am,
each line, each story,
a part of my freedom.

UNFETTERED

I've cut the strings
of others' expectations,
and in this release,
I've found myself—
untethered, unbound,
finally, my own.

HOME WITHIN

I am home within myself,
no longer searching for shelter
in someone else's eyes.
Here, in my own embrace,
I am safe, I am free.

UNSHACKLED

I have unshackled my soul
from past hurts,
from all the stories
I thought I had to carry.
Now, I walk light,
liberated, whole.

FREE SPIRIT

In every breath, I choose freedom,
the kind that comes from knowing
I am enough, whole as I am,
a spirit too wild to cage.

BOUNDLESS

I am boundless,
defined by nothing but my own truth.
In embracing my edges and curves,
I have found the freedom
to be just as I am.

WINGS

I gave myself permission
to unfurl, to rise,
to let the weight fall away.
Now, with wings unbroken,
I soar into my own light.

SELF-EMBRACE

In the arms of my own love,
I have found peace.
No need to search elsewhere—
I am complete,
a universe within.

WHOLEHEARTED

I live with my heart open,
no longer guarding its softness,
embracing each beat
as proof of my freedom,
of my choice to be whole.

NO APOLOGIES

I no longer apologize
for taking up space.
I am here, unashamed,
a full, wild, untamed self,
and that is enough.

OPEN SKIES

I have released the need
to be anything other
than what I am.
Under open skies,
I stand whole,
a part of everything.

UNBOUND JOY

Joy needs no permission.
I laugh freely,
dance wildly,
for I am complete,
and this happiness
belongs only to me.

SELF-WOVEN

I have woven myself
from the threads of my past,
my dreams, my truths.
Now I am a tapestry whole,
crafted by my own hands.

LIBERATION

In releasing who I thought
I had to be,
I discovered freedom—
a lightness in my soul,
an unbreakable peace.

UNCHAINED HEART

My heart is unchained,
loving without walls,
without fear of what comes next.
I am whole, open,
and unafraid to feel.

TRUE TO ME

I am free,
not by anyone's gift,
but by my own choice—
to live, to love,
to be true to who I am.

UNBREAKABLE

Nothing can take this from me—
the wholeness I have claimed,
the freedom I have found.
I am unbreakable,
a light untamed.

ECHOES OF FREEDOM

In every step,
I feel the echoes of freedom,
the peace of being
exactly as I am meant to be,
nothing more, nothing less.

WHOLE AS I AM

I need nothing added,
nothing removed.
I am whole as I am,
a complete being,
at peace with my flaws,
with my light.

CLAIMED AND FREE

I have claimed myself,
in every broken piece,
every beautiful edge.
In this ownership,
I am free, whole,
exactly as I choose to be.

FREEDOM OF SELF

To be free is to be whole,
complete in each choice,
each breath.
In owning yourself,
you find liberation.

LIGHT AS AIR

There is a lightness
in being true—
a weight lifted,
a joy found
in simply being.

CLAIMED FREEDOM

Claim your freedom,
the right to live fully,
to laugh loudly,
to dance without care.
In each choice,
you declare yourself whole.

A Note on the Author

Dina Ezzeddine is a writer and illustrator from Canada. Dina has a degree in Visual Arts and Design, as well as a Bachelor of Arts degree in English. Dina has written numerous children's book and numerous teen books. This book of poetry is her latest work. You can find more of Dina's upcoming work online!

Find more of Dina's here:
visit Amazon & Barnes & Noble

◉ author_cksmith
✉ aiko10195@gmail.com
ⓕ CKSmithAuthor

LEAVE US A REVIEW!

☆☆☆☆☆

Give us your opinions and thoughts
on any of our works!
Wherever books are sold!

IN THIS COLLECTION
GRAB YOUR COPY TODAY!

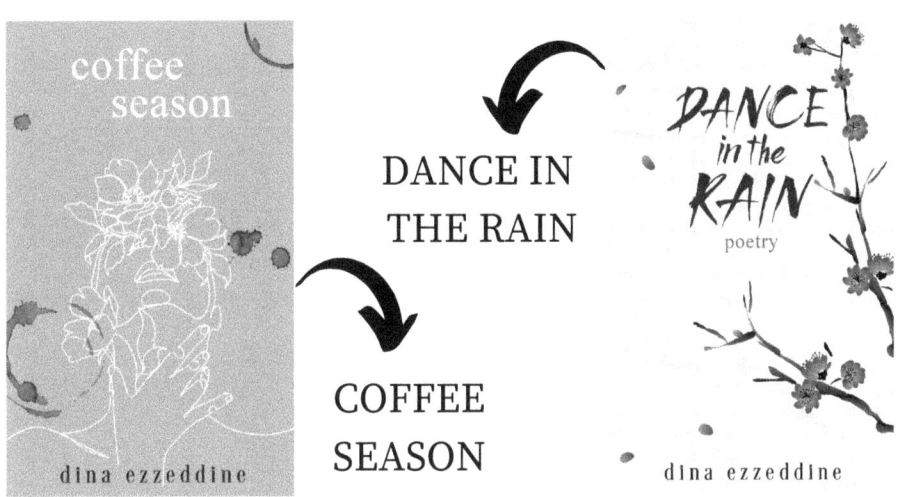

DANCE IN THE RAIN

COFFEE SEASON

THINGS I CAN'T SAY

SEASONS IN BLOOM

AMAZON, BARNES & NOBLE, COLES/INDIGO BOOK STORES & EVERYWHERE!

OTHER BOOKS BY THE AUTHOR

CHILDREN'S BOOKS
. Toshi and the missing Ball-y
. Toshi visits London, England
. Toshi visits Pairs, France
. Toshi in Tokyo
. Toshi and his human sisters

TOSHI AND THE MISSING BALL-Y

OUT NOW! GRAB YOUR COPY!

SAM COOPER HATES BULLIES

Samantha Cooper, a 10-year-old girl who refuses to be intimidated by the school bully, meets Tiffany Simmons. When Samantha begins a new school, Tiffany and her gang make her life miserable, but Samantha's determination to stand up for herself and others leads her to an unlikely ally. Sam meets Max, and Nate, two quiet school nerds, who has been bullied by Tiffany. Together, they devise a plan to expose Tiffany's true colors at the school's talent show. However, as they prepare for their big moment, they face unexpected challenges and learn the true meaning of courage, empathy and friendship. Will Sam, Max and Nate's bravery be enough to bring down the school bully and restore peace to the school? Dive into this inspiring tale of self-discovery and empowerment and find out.

GRAB YOUR COPY TODAY

RELEASING SOON!! AMAZON, and Barnes & Noble and all e-book platforms.

www.ingramcontent.com/pod-product-compliance
Lightning Source LLC
Chambersburg PA
CBHW040801150426
42811CB00056B/1113